GLASSFUL OF PRAYER

Praise for Glassful of Prayer

In *Glassful of Prayer*, his debut book of poems, Anthony Ceballos weaves together stories of family and community, loss and love. From the first poem to the last, he offers prayers of blessing for his mother and grandmother, prayers for the loss of his absent father, poems in praise of the Minneapolis neighborhood where he grew up, and poems of praise and supplication to the earth. In *Sing*, he sings until he cannot sing any more. And in, *Listen, the Earth*, he says "this is the earth/her voice will guide us home." *Glassful of Prayer* is a deeply moving collection of poems.

- **Carolyn Holbrook, Author of** *Tell Me Your Names* **and** *I Will Testify*

Alive with tangible longing, the poems in *Glassful of Prayer* make music of loss. Here, though Ceballos tethers the reader to "the scattered Kodak family" in this "end-time colonial settler nightmare," he simultaneously claims the power of poetry to heal. The poet becomes "Geppetto building. . . with words and letters." The moving poems in *Glassful of Prayer* remain haunted by a "father still / at the bottom of basement stairs," and the speaker sees themselves as "the splintered bedlam" of reflection. Ceballos fills the pages with the hypnotic membering of the poet's body, and declares: "The poets lungs are a rebellion." Yes. Listen to this poet's "bel canto."

-**Kimberly Blaeser, author of** *Ancient Light* **& past Wisconsin Poet Laureate**

Glassful of Prayer
by Anthony Ceballos

Copyright © Feburary 01, 2026 Anthony Ceballos

No part of this book may be used or performed without written consent of the author, if living, except for critical articles or reviews.

Ceballos, Anthony
1st edition

ISBN: 978-1-949487-53-4
Library of Congress Control Number: 2025945750

Interior design by Natasha Kane
Cover design by Joel W. Coggins
Editing by Kris Bigalk and Sophie Baker

Trio House Press, Inc.
Minneapolis
www.triohousepress.org

for my mother & grandmother

Table of Contents

Sing   3

I

Mortal Thread   7
Shot   8
Land/Body   9
Until We Meet Again   11
When the Body Wages Without Breath   16
Word & Thread   18
By These Waters   19
Mother of the Splintered Bench   20
The Day the Poems Failed Us   22
Body of Earth   23
Scattered   24
Hair   26
Unsettling   28

II

Death of the Father   33
Glassful of Prayer   34
My Father Was Called by the Same Name   36
Urge   37
canticum in fine terra   38
Father/Time   40

III

Listerine Dream   45
Ghost   46
Desire   47
Until the Light   48

spiral. down.	50
No Lazarus	51
strange sleep	52
Fingertip & Palm	53
612	54
Mirroring	57
What Is Will Always Be	58
Two Lungs	61

IV

Maybe Extinguished Son	65
Eastbound Twenty-One	67
Gratitude	68
The Hands of Two Brown Men	70
In Winter Along the Weathered Curb	71
Mercy	72
an exhalation	74
at dawn, bel canto	75
Listen, the Earth	76
Southside Coffee Shop	77
River's Grace	78
Good Night Hunter	79
River Call	80

Author's Note	83
Acknowledgments	87
About the Author	91

Sing

It came down the road one night.
It came over the water, across the sky.
It came in a needle, it poured from a bottle.
Along the shore I found a shell, held it
to my ear and yes I could hear it there.
My mother's voice was not her own,
but a moth's that sang a tuneless lullaby.
It tore the leaves from trees, left them
scattered on the cold cement, everything
was ice, frozen in the middle of a second,
and all the sparrows and doves began to fall
away from heaven, should our heavens be,
as I stood where the road reaches water,
as it shrouded Earth in an endless squall,
and I sang for the sun I could not find.
I sang for my mother a gentle lullaby.
I sang for the sparrow and the dove.
I sang for the sky, sang for the shore,
the trees and all their scattered leaves.
I sang until I could sing no more.

I.

Mortal Thread

a single thread of fabric unravels,
now he rends his own impermanence,
his family and the hourglass, how it claims
by surprise, anguish of a drained spirit,
uncle, hotel room, 7th floor apartment,
grandmother, another uncle, a father still
at the bottom of a flight of basement stairs,
all pulled into a formless ocean, call it
a great swallow or the faded shore or
a lunar moth adrift, above the tide,
toward inferno, this temple of flame
like coal, acid, midnight's final drop
of siphoned blood, eviscerates flesh,
fabric, a single lucid thread raveled off
Actuality's cloak or just his perception
of lumination's reflection across a stage,
now the costumes, props and sets,
the cones, rods, curtains, house, ignite,
an entirety so hot all that remains is cold
nothing if nothing can truly be, in here
a cello's lorn canto drops without resolve,
a cloud of vitreous stream, the hollowed
arid spheres that once contained worlds,
a long wave to ash, dust, he will kneel
before the door of mortal night,
in his rage against a faded light,
a faded day, a fated sight.

Shot

I swallowed a bullet at twenty-one,
it came in a shot glass, didn't make a sound,
slowly eroded my spine, its numbness
caught me by surprise as I folded myself,
fetal position, over me, an upturned spirit,
as it was above, so it shall below,
invitation, incinerated throat,
esophagus, gripped by Achlys,
the thread that stitched an eye,
sewn shut so all that I would see,
a grandmother's hand on the casket of a son,
another son, not once but twice she says goodbye,
says *I'll be there soon* and the last son left,
will break through a locked apartment door,
will see the scattered Kodak family,
will know she is with his brothers once more,
& his sister, her daughter, my mother,
I see the plum of cloth and bruise,
a beloved blouse as you face away
from the camera, dice potatoes at the counter,
a family's only Christmas, there your only boy,
your key, your reminder of a man,
days of wine, days of rose,
& here my father frozen
beneath a prayer of snow,
bottom of someone's basement stairs,
a silence I've held through every season,
fatherless child, single Ojibwe mother,
and twenty years later, as a doctor says
*remove the colon, watch the lymph nodes,
here's what we do*, a bullet swallowed alone,
it came in a shot glass & yellowed her skin,
it came in a shot glass & colonized
her body, it came in a shot glass,
it didn't make a sound.

Land/Body

Seven in the morning, an alarm
goes off, I wake within this body,
this sum of every ancestor walked
before, after, this NDN's apocalypse,
once among the birch, cedar, sage, elm,
maple, sweetgrass, now, awake in 2024,
see the soil turn to dust, apparition
of water, life or death, fire or light,
for whom is tomorrow an offer?
Now my nokomis, she reaches out
to take my hand and pulls me into
an embrace I haven't felt in almost
twenty years and time is a vial filled
with salt, and mishomis I remember
when once you told your only daughter
she did a good job raising her only son,
but here, I can't find myself anymore,
I've lost the path and road, it's faded,
manipulated by chimookimaan,
pale death says I should be grateful
for all he's allowed me to keep, says
this land is your land, this land is mine,
what's a little land between old friends?
I see the empty pages of a fifth grade textbook,
the lesson a lie in benevolence come ashore,
at dissonance with a mother left to wonder
what it's like to be okay she thinks,
this drink will have to do instead.
Seven in the morning alarm goes
off in a dream I stumble home again,
back to rivers, lakes, color of sky blue
water, red earth, brown earth, this earth,
more than survival, more than any
white-out dragged across unerasable
truth, that this country loves to destroy,
to banish away what isn't convenient,
the rusted cage and razor wire gavel,

suits on capitol hill who prey,
they pray this truth will go away,
go away go away just go away!
I hear a bully bark at dream's end,
seven in the morning, I wake up,
this body and land, my body
and land, call it truth,
call it home.

Until We Meet Again

I

In the 1990s, a mother hides her body's tremor
behind a box on a shelf in a breaking kitchen cabinet,
and somewhere, a father carries himself back inside
the only Polaroid I have of him, he buries himself
beneath a bunch of letters and forms, a drawer
in a long gone desk given to charity or trash
and now an only son seals himself within
a bottle of water or wine, prescription pills,
he cries *throw me far from shore! Far, far away!*

II

In 2020, sister pulls up to the curb in a beat up white suv,
asks her brother how he's doing and later will ask her boyfriend
for a little more help, will pray to God for a little more time.
In her hands I saw our mother's hands again, and again,
way back there, a cousin dies when a car rolls over,
somewhere, only he knows, only sixteen, his sister,
a girl my age with two kids on the rez will tell herself
tomorrow has to be better than today, but today
was always a gift we were never promised.

III

Way back then in a Duluth hotel room, an uncle let go
his final breath on a bed next to a woman he called
his love, or maybe just his or maybe justice dissolves
beneath the tongue, a word I let fall slowly from the edge
of my lips call it nitrate vasodilator or nitroglycerin as in
not enough his mother says *he had a heart attack*
his sister hears, refuses to believe, sinks herself
to the bottom of a bottle of Windsor Canadian Whiskey,
worn Brooks and Dunn tape, her own discordant howl.

IV

My grandmother is a constellation. In my dreams,
she visits all the time, tells me I'm still her number one,
asks me about her beloved daughter as we sit inside
her Franklin Avenue apartment on the seventh floor,
as we sit inside my childhood apartment on Minnehaha,
number two-oh-one until I drop back into my body,
two-thousand-twenty-four years away from patient zero,
thirty-four years as a congregation of every echo,
here are my hands, here is my skin, these are my eyes
the sunlight finds through half turned dusty blinds.

V

Today in a bathroom mirror I couldn't see myself,
the way I need, my reflection, eyes, lips, teeth,
skin and every deep line I've whispered into being,
who am I when all of them are on another side, I am
therefore a poem bursts through concrete and dirt,
therefore a body of work or the work of a body,
how my hands command our glass to pieces, I
finally see myself along the splintered bedlam,
I only know I am when we fall in heavy fragments.

When the Body Wages Without Breath
after Rosy Simas 'she who lives on the road to war'

     oh my mother, nimaamaa,
   every movement a journey
across an earth we no longer
recognize, a world no longer ours,
that weeping willow I remember
  from across Minnehaha Avenue, vanished,
    just like the water, butterflies & bees,
              where have they all gone?
  the soil is dust in my grandfather's hands,
  that old red road is littered with maps
of war, fire & oil in a colonizer's font,
meticulous, chimookimaan's lust
  for disintegration, I hear you mother, you say
                 no more
         a lullabye, soft, in a dream,
    I hear you beg me to rest,
   we've been on the run for too long,
  too far across a minefield of our bodies erased,
 our tongues redacted, our dance twisted,
tied around pledges, prayer not our own.
rest   I hear you say from the edge
of an entirety I'm not sure is real anymore,
but in my blood, I feel a pulse, a rhythm,
 this connection delicate as a silken thread,
 born of Milky Way, this thread to keep
  mother to son, daughter to mother,
   to sister, brother, uncle, niece & aunty,
    to granddaughter, grandson, grandfather,
   oh grandmothers who spin this world,
  oh, Earth Mother as she is all & she
tends to fire, manoomin, berries,
   cedar smoke & sweetgrass, you say
       see how our turtle rests beneath Orion's night,
       how every direction leads to center, home,

I hear you, from the edge of a dream,
nookomis I remember your voice,
your body a prayer, gichi-manidoo,
I keep a bag of tobacco in my backpack,
 place a pinch down to tell you I'm okay,
  nimaamaa, gidaanis,
   she's hanging on, better
    than she's been, tells me
     you'd be proud of us both,
     proud of me, proud of her,
    & it gives me just enough hope
   I let my body rest for a minute,
  I let my body rest, breathe,
 for a minute, I let my body
rest, breathe, our bodies,
 just for a minute,
  let them rest,
   let them
    breathe.

Word & Thread

any page or any drop of ink,
any heartbeat or what is mine isn't
mine, a thread of irregular rhythm,
this hymn for a city by the river,
sing a note from the skeleton key,
i will wash away my body's grief,
in these immaculate sky blue waters,
this font this curve of ink made blood,
i will smear my hands across the canvas,
wait for an echo of sound and skin,
midnight's sleep upon the open book,
any thread of any page i will unravel.

By These Waters

Oh my father, vent the flood in my head,
my brain is too drenched, drowned
in ungodly spirit, wet as my pillowcase
when my eyes reveal another sun,
when my hand opens blinds the brilliance
overwhelms, I think my body is on fire.
Oh mother, help me find home in the ultraviolet,
my capillaries hide an ultraviolence,
my childhood fingers threw the Rubik's
down a long stairwell, all the small pieces,
if I can't follow the form, examine the parts
that build up the body, oh sister,
your body, this body, our bodies.
My body houses an uncle's old drinking song,
Brooks & Dunn's "Neon Moon," I wander
beneath its ionized glow & hum,
while these beat up dreams, they stumble,
lay their broken bones across the beams.
Oh my mother, my father, my sister, my sister,
it'll be alright, in the light I'll repent,
let my pen confess all these sins,
wash myself in the baptismal font,
blessed my this water poured onto dirt.

Mother of the Splintered Bench

      my   mother
    is all   of Minneapolis
   wilted   on every bus bench
    shrouded in scarves   coats   hood
     tight over her head to   protect hide
     these are two   of the same goal
     and her hands   notice her hands
    how they shake   as she grips
   her walker   struggle up a curb
   little cart   of everything or
nothing or a bottle   pills   liquor
whatever slows   the tremble
my mother is all   of Minneapolis
and i am the bad son   *always have been*
 is what i tell myself   for every year
  of her long spiral   favorite direction
   down where gravity   drags a heart
    down to the ground we'll always meet
     low   a bad bad son   i'll always be
      always   a chance to do
       more   good maybe
        another   dollar or
         phone   call or
          what you are

```
                or a question
              as in what's left
           to offer is it all just sinew
        what more can I give of me before
     i am no longer whole was it understood
      i would give        have given myself away
      to save anyone      who wouldn't be saved
      with this i carry   my own lost pieces
      only ever seen              inside a mirror
      when i think              it's her reflection
      all across                    Minneapolis
      am i the one she sees     or is she the sea
      by which we seek          to see and be seen
      i watch her face             as it passes by
      dead stare                  from another side
      filthy scratched              bus window
      here i am                      i am here
      unholy son                  wilted all over
      this city                   this splintered
      death                                 bench
```

The Day the Poems Failed Us
(after Martín Espada's "The Republic of Poetry")

My mother called me one day to politely ask
if poems fell from the sky. She caught one
on her tongue that morning walking to a store
or a bar from a house for wayward Indians.

Before I could answer, the line went dead.
The snow was static, was ash, was a question
I could not answer, not in english, not with words,
not a thing I could do but plead mercy through a pen.

This poem - no balm for a woman beneath the influence.
This son - his hands in finality close an apartment door.
This oxygen - our breath is sheathed in nicotine and lead.
This water - we no more shall drink, oh unholy libation.

My mother called me in great distress one morning,
a poem was caught in her throat.

Body of Earth

If this body is composed of Earth,
I refuse to become a cloud of ash
or a dervish of devil's dust or allow
my blood to be siphoned, my veins
drilled to quench the serpent tongue.
The spit of these words will never not fall.
This skin will not give way to eroded desert.
My hands will not be cast in polyethylene.
My arms will not embrace the leaded weight,
augury of death. These teeth will not masticate
the scattered carrion, all this wasted life, nature,
wasted in the name of some ruby, diamond dog,
but this body carved of Earth will not be razed
nor these bronchial forests reduced to cinder.
There will be no fever dream, no sky inflamed.
Here is my mother, her body composed of Earth.
Here is my father, his body composed of Earth.
Here is my grandmother who gave us light.
In every eye, silver dawn, the obsidian night,
deeper now, past the lens, a vitreous sea,
like water, is water, the body and the Earth.

Scattered

        i remember   my grandmother's hands
            brown sculptures   curved index finger   pointing
                  my direction   telling me
have patience   *good things come*   *to those*   *who aren't messy eaters*
        my uncles weather   worn skin gravel   in their
                                      voices
    cousins playing   in the yard   my mother   my sisters
  my apartment   *201*   on Minnehaha Avenue
        shag   green carpet   mailbox with tape
                & my father's   last name *my*
                      father
            fallen warrior   journey home
        stopped
  by glass   caught in the throat
      whiskey   on scarred tongue
    body frozen on cement   bones shattered
          i remember   the bus shelter
    broken bench
across the street   grass   overgrown   on thirty-third
      windows   closing at night   an elevator
        that hummed   softly   quiet
                work   song
    any time   any one   needed lift   i
remember my grandfather   glasses & ponytail
    his nickname for me   *charlie*
        brown
i remember when he told my mother *you did a good job raising him*
    she remembers this too
       back in the day   when phones
                hung on walls
   looking up my last name   in a phone book wondered
if my father   would answer   any of those numbers   i
    remember this
  toy boxes   drawing pads
   crayola watercolors   permission slips
     report cards & backpacks barely clinging
      to my shoulders   math worksheets
    that still make me sweat   the middle of night

horror of long division   haunting me   into adulthood
                      i remember   not having to remember
         everything just   was   in the moment
                   now i remember   remembering
   looking   back
             things that made me   once   part of life   now
                        part of history
                            when *is*   becomes
                was
            was   is a noun   a thing i cling to   cannot hold
         cannot help   but remember.

Hair

When I first cut off my long dark mane back in 2012,
I wanted the world to see the man I never had growing up,
rough boy, angular features, never taught how to throw a punch,
warrior, soldier, someone who would've made my uncles proud,
cowboy that would've brought my father back from the dead,
taken the vodka from his veins, poured it back into the bottle
screwed the cap on tight and tossed the bottle away from us,
that's what I wanted when I chopped my long dark mane,
        clean cut,   straight lines,   fresh portrait.

When my hair met my eyes, I still felt like a boy, not quite
a man, but that shaggy fella who was afraid if you looked
him in the eye you'd see all he despised about himself,
regrets, failures, broken bottles and arguments with other
gay boys he told himself he loved, told him it was love for who
could resist the charm of an early-twenties mop top, bruised ego
        one-way   trip to sanitarium, cranium cracked,
     held by protein,   skull stitched together.

When my hair fell past my chin, I think I forgot about being
a boy or a man, David Bowie on repeat, intrigue of in-between,
not quite male, not quite female, silhouette of androgyny, thrill
of other men not able to make heads or tails, back or front
of this unfathomable subject walking too close to their body,
their temple, their church of a heteronormative Jesus,
with a fantasy to grip, to pull midnight's river cascading
from my head   maybe solve their own mysteries,
       quell their own   insecurities,

sent to the embrace of a man who told me I was only my hair,
made me something desirable, not a word nor whisper, nor love
without exception, all tossed at a wall and dropped from ghosts' hands,
but an image I cast and the rest just junk found damaged at a goodwill,
caked in dust, lovable from a distance if you squint your eyes enough
still I let my hair grow past my shoulders, thought I could wrap each
strand around his body, keep him   at my side,   but I woke,
        in the middle of the night   gasping for air   frayed   split

and when my hair got to my chest, I sat next to my mother
in a sanitized doctor's office, gripping those strands between my fingers,
hearing words like   *lymph nodes*   *survival rates*   *remove the colon*
life drained from the room, through the vents, light switch, crack
beneath the door and I thought of my mother months later,
would her own hair fall before her sickness fell, Ojibwe woman,
no reflection, head wrapped in scarves, decay, I imagined
grabbing the scissors on the desk, chopping off my long dark mane,
     sacrifice to any god   buzzing in the fluorescents overhead.

Unsettling
after Rosy Simas "weave"

you   are my sister,
you   are my brother,
you   are my mother,
you   my father bid to be a father,
you   are my breaking bones,
my need   to drown in the womb,
be reborn   as an already dead rose,
through dirt   on an earth not on fire,
this land   this native's apocalypse, this
your flesh ungendered   your body   unsexed,
my hair around your hair, our eyes sewn shut,
as we swim through tar, through molten rock,
through a split in our skin,   a split through
time   through air, through fog and you
you   who are my sister,
you   who are my brother, my mother,
my father bid to be my father,
    shoot thorns from your tongue,
    watch their bibles go up in flames,
their english reduced to an ash
our relations will whorl away
    with a single breath
    we will not be silent, we
    were never meant to be silenced,
        they sharpen their knives,
    aim for eye and tongue,
but we will not be spilled
as we claw our way back home,
every variation, us descendants,
us enrolled, us twenty-three-point five percent,
us sixty-seven percent, full blood, half blood, this blood,
reservation, inner-city, high schooled, college schooled,
no schooled, boarding schooled, with our fathers, without
our fathers, our mothers in hospital beds, our mothers
in nursing homes, our mothers in agony, we
will weave our stories together
& end this end-time colonial settler nightmare
they call am■i■

II

Death of the Father

is death of the eyes, hands, skin,
the tongue, teeth, voice, soft tissue,
the nervous system, respiratory system,
all his systems failed by the cruelty
of American systems, acid, esophagus,
stomach lining, one lung rots, now two,
all gone, death of air & water, disappeared,
the oceans, rivers, elms, trillium & goldenrod,
the bittered sweetgrass, oh wrathful Helios,
this is an absent light at the end of the world,
this is an absent man from the beginning of life,
this is a death in the home, the family, the brain,
death of the eardrum as it hears vertebrae snap,
this is one way a father can die, bottles piled
on bottles, piled on bottles, blood & body,
here is what we lose to dirt: man & men,
children of men or the only child of a man,
this is the death of an unhappy marriage,
these are the voices a mother hears at night,
silence on the line, in the line, a pocket,
breath where breath should never be,
attack on a heart tacked to the wall,
dropped receiver, now the line is dead,
now a father and son fade to carbon,
this was the senior who begat a poet,
whose name was a legacy of blank paper,
who embraced the azure until it burned,
until it became a cloud of Acherontia.
Father, this is how I speak of death,
as ash erupted from my mouth,
my voice, all you have left.

Glassful of Prayer

There's nothing there, all
the relics have disappeared,
no overflowed shot across the counter,
no forgotten bottle, half emptied,
under the bed, no rusted ax to split
my head, every guilt drenched morning,
whiskey soaked week,
wine blotted year, losing my breath
    beneath the unwater, I inhale.
    Oh, holy libation.
    Oh, blood the color of grapes & cherries.
    Oh, father of vodka perspiration.
Oh my father, who stained the spiked edge of glass,
one fall, one night, the bottom of the stairs,
how death tied the blindfold,
how morning refused to greet you.
See, mourning found a son instead,
seeped through mangled, dusty blinds
with a light too bright, so bright
I swore I was floating
above a Minneapolis on fire until I dropped,
        pulled through a makeshift sky,
        clouds of ash and dust,
        wreckage of once was,
        back to land with a hazy crash,
        body on sweat stained sheets.
        Swore I saw you, my father,
        on the way down,
        but it was just my reflection,

in the window, next to the bed,
some branches, a warm summer breeze,
clock that says it's 2:13 pm & me
telling myself *shhhh, it's nothing,*
or was it you telling me *it's something,*
just close your eyes & count to three
one   two   three

> *it will all get better*
> *if you fall*
> *back to drink.*

My Father Was Called by the Same Name

Now, I am called. Listen.
Does it transfuse my blood
with aromatic bitter or is it just
a fissure, infected, red that weeps
golden if I hold a pen too tight?
Tight enough to call a pulse
a prayer to bring you back,
though I know no incantation
has yet to stop the falling scythe
or reverse the irreversible cessation
of all your biological functions.
Listen, someone wants to reach you,
but it's my body that sways to the ring.
Instead, have I had a chance to tell you?
Death is the distance that separates
who we are, but you still are.
My father. I am your only son.
Look. In my hands I hold a name.
Ours. This proper noun we share.
Oh how you follow me still.

urge

    crystal bottles

             aluminum cans

dissonance

      he can't

              control

shot

    in the mouth

          a shot

      down the throat

   in a glass

      to the head

father

    save him

      your holy son

        his breaking neck

            the glory of

canticum in fine terra

He slumbers on the wilted bench.
He warms against a crystal drift.
He waits in sorrow for an unarrival,
for a butterfly, a bird and bee.
He waits for a pale horse's beat,
for the white shroud of surrender,
for the crane of a burdened sky,
for the blood sunfall, how long
will midnight draw its breath?
He washes it down, the green veil.
He washes it down, the bar between
nowhere, here, alive and alive,
all the bricks drawn in red,
the bond, the burden and the son
of a starless night, wandered
darkness settles in his lungs,
infects the open mouth, throat,
tongue, air way, windpipe, acid,
acidic, acidity, a city, infection,
in ruins, an acid city infected.
Weight of the inverted hourglass.
Weight of the glass sanded hour.
Weight of a steel bolted minute.
Weight of stolen time, stolen
clouds into petrol, siphoned
from the weight of the font,
weight of water, how long
can the river wait, how long?
The golden rod is ash.

The trillium is ash.
The willow weeps ash.
The ashen angel weeps death.
Radio Heaven, confirmation;
this is Radio Hell all around him,
in front of him, the molten clock,
before his eyes, a face.
there isn't going back
there isn't going back
there isn't coming
or going from here
there isn't h　re
the　e isn't th　re
t　e　e i　't us
　　　　isn't you.

Father/Time

(In January of 2022, Bulletin of the Atomic Scientists announced humanity was only 100 seconds away from midnight...a.k.a. armageddon)

my father is a broken clock
his gears rusted   his face
glass   shatter   clishhhhhhhhh
scatter the fragments   ashes   fragmented
memories   [24:60]   decomposition   [24:60]
                      his heart frozen between
                              [00:00] on/off [00:00]

    he is nowhere anymore
    time is all around me
    he is no more anywhere
    time is all around me
    though the clock is busted
    lip busted   eye busted
    body   busted   mugshot
    found on google
    hi dad!

he is all around me
the watch my mother gave me
ticking away too beautiful to burden

        with the pressure of unexisting
        i refuse to set it don't expect to turn the dial
        don't expect to turn the dial
        don't expect
        the dial
        to turn
        two turns
        the clock is twice right

                [00:00] / [00:00]
                once ante meridian
                once prime meridian
                forward / backward

backward/forward

stop my father
stop   my father
father   stop
him   my father
please   before

a trip down stairs,
day of doom,
a concrete slab,
a crack of vertebrae
day of doom snap
the airway
day of doom
bear the pall

alarm

goes off
goes silent

alarm

          goes

going

gone

tick!
tick!
tick!

[00:00]

III

Listerine Dream

Peppermint please,
or spearmint, winter mint,
gum or candy mint,
      as old lovers, ex-friends
clutch their arms
around me, forget
      my anger as we
      catch up, quick, meet
turn away as one straw
      snaps the camel's spine
& down goes the narrator, I
travel through hazy flowers,
night walks, there's too much
to forget, I have no ID,
no money but watch me,
      a treasure in the medicine
cabinet, poison control,
(the writer) begs two eyes,
how do angels die? (he assumes)
in little rooms with locked doors,
lights on & a vent's drill,
a lid's twitch a monotone death song
      sing it sing it sing it sing
      I (he wails) am a son
of the drunk, cracked statue,
glued together,
at the edge of shatter,
      give up & choke
      on vomit the verge
      of anything or loss
      of everything
I ask, does the sun exist
on the other side of cement?
      (he assumes no)
so smash the face into glass,
shove cardboard spoons down the throat,
weigh the body down with steel,
tell me no one cares,
      at least my breath is fresh.

The Ghost of My Father

The ghost of my father is shrouded in black,
as he enters my room to lead my hand,
down where devils find shape & contour,
down where coins will sing their final refrain.
Forever I have dreamed of meeting him,
but this night time terror only disturbs, unsettles,
so I flee, through a field of open sores,
catching my feet on the vines of rotting grapes
as hands of the dead offer me respite,
solace from the weight of this messy waltz.
My father laughs as he sees me struggle,
whispers to me, *You are my son.*
You are not free of this tradition.
You too will taste a thorn on your tongue.

desire

it's eleven at night
    look at u
        you're d   nk   again
            & every morning   you start

      hung   damp   dizzy   over   a rod
          & there's nomore G d
  to fix
      u
            babyboybabyboy

    no temple two too to tú catch your   prayers
      the sirens   of A.A.   sing   u
        to an edge   you

          drop

eleven at morningnightmorningnightnevernevernever

     you lay your body

                down

             blackout

              to forget

                      every

Until the Light

Hard to describe,
not fire, more like weight
on chest stomach maybe both
replaced by acid, anxiety,
where once an esophagus
held sentinel now long burned
away with every glass of bordeaux red
over the last ten years to sate a gap,
childhood adrift among crushed
beer cans, cigarettes, holes burned
into couches while adults didn't quite sleep,
it looked like sleep but heavier, restless,
without dream, the dreams I called my own
at seven years old, but never mind all that
because this thing hard to describe,
this pressure sucking air from my lungs,
this static replacing my heart gets louder
every time I inhale & I see my grandmother
rise above the earth, eyes filled with tears,
slowly, she opens her mouth,
slowly, she tilts her head,
Who? Who do you want to be?
speaks to me of failure, says she left
me in charge of her only daughter,
an alcoholic I have called my mother,
tells me not to speak   suddenly
a flash   she is gone
and I know this is a nightmare
but I can't tell the difference

until the light of morning
when I jolt myself awake,
can't move, for a few minutes,
I see myself float above,
count to three, shake my arm,
and body follows suit,
and all day I have a headache,
and all day the floor is tilted,
the sun is too bright,
and all day this is what
remains on my chest.

spiral. down.

                      a single line
                    isolation hour
                    open mouth
                of gods or god   *who saw the whirl*
                or some god   *who can't find a way please*
                any god here   *my bones are dust where*
                  is my body   *is the soot that remains*
                    sacrifice   *anything for a hit of you*
                  in isolation   *a single light above my head*
                  a single line   *augury of death i love*
                    you you you   *you you you you*
              consume every part   *the open mouth*
            all this skin erupted   *a blood sky*
        from the mouth of orchids taste   *vanilla wet*
      sweet taste honey taste the petal   *delicate*
    between your teeth i am torn to god   *i fall*
    before his lingering eye he sails
    in through a bedroom window
    second story a buried house
    i walk i strut this predawn hour
      place a single line on my chest
      like a god inhale away my life
        are a god but you choke on it
          my heart in your windpipe
          or the single line all
            you saw clouds
              this weather not
                for you a line
                  crystal drift
                    cold snow

No Lazarus

My father begat an only son,
but I am a mother's son with
out a father so maybe I am
the son of a man, I am not
my father's boy, I am not
his body, I am not nobody
nor no body's blood nor
am I the fall that brought
his hand into death's hand,
betrayed by a false sense
of balance, veins swollen,
acrid spirit and whose face
did father see when Christ
sealed the crystal bottle?
Darkest day of the lost father,
oh I am no man's son, I am
no Lazarus in disguise yet
his left-behind, they preach,
I have his eyes, nose, lips,
all of his face they plead,
in the genes, his DNA,
half of me will always be
my father but spare the son
his sins, for holy is the ghost
who sees his name etched
in another man's grave.

strange sleep

if you find yourself in bed
with a stranger you say you love,

staring at a ceiling, trying to find
meaning in all the little cracks,

leaks, chipping paint, maybe
you've lived, just a little anyway.

turn your head to the left & see a map
of the world against his uncovered back,

while he sleeps you imagine a life
you've never seen, a life you'll never see,

a mountain you'll never climb, your name not a breath
across his lips as you contemplate this dreamlessness.

every rise & fall of his chest the pulse
of an ocean's bottom, the silence of 2 a.m.

impossibilities, to walk across water,
dance with the unbroken, drown,

a hurricane, ribs or femur fractured, fooled
by the fool, the eye, seer of nothing, seer of truth.

if you find yourself in bed with a stranger
and you can't remember love, just close your eyes,

hold your breath, begin to count,
prayer for sleep, quiet, dream.

o n e t w o t h r e e f o u r f i v e s i x

Fingertip & Palm

My skin a corroded silk I wear
for no audience but the apparition
that stares at me from the otherside
of a sunlit pool of reflection, he warns
of a day we will drown beside the tide,
of water ceded to gasoline, ignited, he is
yesterday and tomorrow and here I remain.
Today this skin of mine in memoriam to him,
I have watched it bleed against cold concrete,
I have felt it inflame against nickel and chlorine,
I have scratched it red as a vein of molten Earth
to see myself become a withered desert,
to stand along the precipice of years gone
to sand from the womb of another hourglass
thrown from the husk of tattered Babel,
this skin I cannot save from my own weary eye,
these eyes or his eyes or our eyes, he reaches
to cup his chin in my rusted fingers,
to remember the softness of our youth,
to pull the Marlboro from between our lips
and map the constellations across our face
with fingertip and palm, a prayer of flesh
our hands find through ashen generations
of tissue wilted, starved in time, a shield
we share: this vellum, this swollen tide.

612

(after Allen Ginsberg's "Howl")

I saw the warm spiral of a false chemical paradise,
I saw foil, aluminum, cardboard, prayers to God,
I saw the stagger and fall of divine across cold concrete,
the tattered linen wrapped across a bloodied shoulder,
across another bloodied shoulder hung the veil
of a faded woman, a faded man, fated to the haze
of the foundry of death, I saw midnight claim thorn,
I saw the broken bones of what was once a wing,
a shadow cast from within the unforgiven hill,
I saw the doors of an eastbound bus that never opened,
I saw the open sign of a northern cafe hemorrhage neon,
I saw the key, the lock, the lock and the deadbolt,
the bolt of blue that drew its fractal tattoo and the fire,
the molten centipede's dominion over flooded veins,
I saw the flooded intersection and three butterflies,
I saw three butterflies and a body of ants swarm
the melted ice cream, in its pool I saw my childhood,
a ruined milky hallucination and in my sleep, in a dream,
I saw my grandmother with a cone of her beloved vanilla
on a seat in a Dairy Queen I haven't seen since the 1990s
and I saw one drop, two, three, fall to the bench below
where I held my breath today, boy gone blue to see
any tomorrow, and yesterday I heard the fireworks,
inhaled the strontium, watched red streak across
a Typhon face, the withered obelisk, two inches away
from a scythe brought down by the asphyxiated barrel,
shattered sons and daughters, I saw the wave rise,
I saw a mother cradle empty space, I saw a mother,
she cradled emptiness, she cradled pin and bevel,
she asked nothing of the angel, called to no God,
she cradled emptiness in her arms, her womb,
I saw her and felt my own hands plunge into ash,
dirt, in Minneapolis, it's road construction season
again I watch the tide of orange swell every artery,
every breath speckled with the powdered avenue,
the perfume of promise, liquid asphalt dabbed against
the skin of Earth already inflamed: promise of what?

Of a sleek movement in and out of our days and nights?
Navigation made beauty through jackhammer and drill?
Destruction swallowed whole for an offer of grace?
And yes I know the necessity of these tremors, our duty
to maintenance, to the mix and pour of hole and fracture,
but now the caution tape is brighter than our mourning sun,
now the vein considers surrender where the shadow is long
there all of grace shall fall to the feet of this prophet
I have heard called infrastructure, without regard
to truth or falsehood, it's silhouette drawn in deep
red lines across the pages of a battered Atlas,
the mark of liquid copper and petroleum that burns
through the sole of every wanderer, vestigial petal gone
underneath the tar I can hear tomorrow plead,
I can hear it's hushed hymn over lost soil,
and the roots lose each other to carbon,
to the print of engine and machine,
in a season of orange and yellow caution,
the warning diamond of Minneapolis,
and the wheel as it spins or stops
for the weight of a burdened crane,
and once, my hands found a glass,
or was it plastic, in the back of a cabinet,
or under the cushion of a couch or bed,
at the end of a Lake Street parking lot,
under the azure sky gone to indigo,
under the rhythm of the raven's wing,
and I let my body wrap itself strong
around it's stem, or was it the cap,
and bid myself permission to quench
a mother's thirst or a father's thirst,
generations of a thirst not my own,
nor my family nor my blood but this drought
that stripped away from soil all of life,
forced it into dust, the body and the bodies
returned to ash, and vitriol fell from the hand
of a god or gods to whom I have yet to pray,
and I believed in water, in the plastic or glass
I held strong in a sculpted grip of survival,
and I drank to know heavenly warmth,
I drank to saturate pages, all cracked,

I drank to live but suffered the rise
of a concrete death through cranium,
the hand that worshiped fractured and cast,
and every verse I sank as holy, as water clear,
dried copper against my shirt, my matted hair.
Oh mother of that heavenly warmth,
oh father and your godlike call to repeat
the list of sins tucked into your breast pocket,
who signals to the sun or son the sum
of every summoned saint we will never be,
of every saint spinning the stars,
or the splattered paint across the north,
at night I see you through polluted sky
you reach for me and though I turn away
I will reach for you again,
we will reach for each other
through neon clouds
of moth and spider's silk,
oh mother, this midnight
is too dark without your lull,
oh father, this breath is shallow
without the voice I've never heard,
and last night I saw two men curve
their bodies against one another,
oh holy the embrace, holy the skin
that finds the heat of another man's skin,
holy the lost transfer, holy the bus bench,
holy the glass shelter and the cigarette
as holy as the flame passed between hands,
holy our great recovery, holy our great fall,
holy the morning that refuses to wake,
holy yesterday, holy tomorrow,
holy the uncertainty, the long shadow,
the unforgiven light and the wing
of a single raven resurrected.
Holy its beat.
Holy its beat.
Holy its beat.

Mirroring

In the glass of a Nicollet storefront,
a body is reflected, one vested as my own
by others near who have seen me turn away,
a body I've learned to claim; my own blood,
my aging skin, bones, spine, acid scarred
esophagus, tobacco stained lungs, kidneys,
liver, organ called a spleen, my father's nose,
my mother's downturned lips, oh saboteur,
this apocalyptic truth, face of a clock ticks,
six seconds ahead of where I never am,
now it's five, now it's four, now is a face
I see reflected over my shoulder, a man,
a voice, he says, *look what you've become.*
    He is my own, caught three seconds ahead
now two won't wait, how long until I believe
I'm the one we see in this Nicollet glass?
I scan our body every night, look down,
crane neck, audit back, enough
of this wet machine, real, enough
to feel each stone, break, fissure.
I've never seen my face, we've never
laid eyes upon our own, just pixels,
a Polaroid or Googled mugshot,
a video, the only evidence I know
that my body exists on this planet,
though time moves faster, our face
remains in perfect step with mine,
with what I think I see, I think I am,
one mirror removed from truth,
one second away from him.

What Is Will Always Be
for my father & his brother

★

The father of a wannabe poet plummets down a flight one day. Smash. Whiskey. Gin. Going. Gone. Fractures his neck and finds heaven or hell, or Heaven or Hell. His brother, not at home, rushes for the hospital, fast as he can, speed limits be damned, only to be stopped head on by another car. *Crash!* There goes the sound of crunching metal. *Crash!* There goes his brother running from police at two in the morning and there on a hospital bed, hooked to a life support machine, rests the father of a wannabe.

The next day, somewhere in South Minneapolis, the future wannabe-poet, son of a man consumed by silence, nephew of a car wrecked head on, sits near his single Ojibwe-from-Mille-Lacs mother on a shag green carpet in a two bedroom apartment on Minnehaha Avenue. He has no idea his father is dead. He has no idea the snap of bone against a concrete floor has extinguished any chance of meeting a man he might have called dad, a man after which he was named, junior to a senior, echo of another son eroded, drowned by the cold fingers of unbottled spirits.

I am not a good poet, I will tell you, sitting at a keyboard in the year 2020, still in Minneapolis, still wondering what my would-be father's voice might have sounded like, trying to write the feeling of never meeting him out of my bones, my blood, my nervous system. No, I am no good poet. Is poetry synonymous with person? If I am not a good poet, am I a bad person? An even worse son?

★

wannabe wannabe oh a wannabe father brother wannabe poet wannabe member of society good friend to few wannabe book snob intellectual politico wanna learn a new language but don't think i ever could cuz i wanna have a better attention span but can't afford the pills wanna handle money better but there was never money to begin wannabe a better Ojibwe but i'll never be enrolled call it quantum physics wannabe a man's man but my voice gets too high wannabe a glamorous actress but my apotheosis falls short and my posture too low wannabe a Captain Picard but my Enterprise is made of paper and i'm afraid of dying in the dark i am afraid of dying in the dark i am afraid i am damned if he has spoken this is all i've ever been

Look at Earth, it's getting smaller. Look at Earth, it's getting further away. Look at me! I'm out of oxygen. Look at me! I'm floating away. Look at my mother, her cancer is gone, her colon is gone, her home is gone. Look at my grandmother making frybread in heaven, my grandpa giving me five dollars. I was a good kid. I was a good child. I was. I was. I was. I. I. I. Was is a noun. I was. I was. Nothing.

I thought I'd be nothing until something until I became a poet, not a doctor, lawyer, astronaut, but Geppetto building the child I never was with words and letters, harmony and dissonance, how the tongue hits the teeth, how the eye sees empty space, deep space, line space, how a hand turns the page as I grip the hollow fold I was nineteen years old when my father's brother reached out through Facebook to say *I held you as a baby!* I was twenty-six years old when I asked him for a few extra dollars cuz I was hungry, tired, between paychecks and he said yes without exception cuz I was his nephew and he told me I never had to explain myself to him I never had to explain.

★

Maybe I'll never know what it is to not be poor, and maybe you'll never read these words. I accept this possibility, accept this sorrow you may never see as I accept this life with a father I will never meet, as you do a life with a brother whose voice will never speak again. These are cruelties that thrash around like immortal beasts when our mortal bodies are upended, but here too is our familial communion: Maybe we both believe this would-be father-once-brother watches over from somewhere beyond the sun and rain, maybe we both feel he is finally at peace as we see him when we see each other. Maybe in its own way, this too is immortality.

★

Two Lungs

plead for an end to my nicotine addiction,
protest with a rite of wheeze and cough,
threaten to cinch any air I drag in a day
watch me stumble in the pallid blue miasma
of every Marlboro or American Spirit at home
between my lips, will not allow my disrespect.
These lungs of mine remind me I've got only one
body in this life as they conference with my heart,
plan their scold and scald, their grievous litany,
they do not stutter, "give us a breath of oxygen,
pure, immaculate, tear yourself free and away
from big tobacco's grip, see poor health run,
it runs in your family, see your mother, father,
grandmother and grandfather, uncles, cousins,
diabetes, arrhythmia, inflammation of nerves,
joints, colon, heart, us, how we grow inflamed
by the minute, by the day with you, don't dig us
an early grave, one body, one life, this breath."
The poet's lungs are a rebellion, this poet's eyes
are off in the clouds, this poet's brain is a frayed
mess of live wire, and his hands, they are tools
for a desperate saboteur, as they thumb heavy
through my bright blue backpack, sharp
for the lighter they will always find.

IV

Maybe Extinguished Son
for Ray

Last night, in a restless sleep
beneath sweat stained sheets,
red comforter, unraveled, endless,
grey wool blanket my mother gave
to me, I saw you there, in a dream.
You said it was me you wanted to find,
we were in some city, some apartment,
so tired, derelict, cold and lifeless,
everything shrouded in dust.
You believed in the possibility
that somehow I could help you
find another way back home.
You spoke of an infinite needle,
of time and how it swallows itself
by the light of our faded days,
you wept ferocious tears,
you ran to me, held me tight,
begged me to bring you back home.
Why you chose me, I don't know,
but I wept with you, heavy sobs,
no room left for oxygen between
our lungfuls of this surrender.
I knew you for forty-five days,
briefly we shared a world away
from our own worlds, old worlds
in exchange for steps into the new,
two moths along the glass bottom,
at the end of a long drink, barely
alive, maybe ours was a thirst
unquenchable, maybe we were
two sons almost extinguished,
or maybe none of it matters,
my human need for reason,
because there you stood,
held yourself up, a fever dream,
a ray of sunshine, clouded, hazy,
ready to ignite the skies

of those who loved you
one more time,
one more chance,
just please help me
find my way back.
In a dream I said I would.
In a dream I told you *breathe,*
you're okay now, I'm here.
I told you. I told you. I told you.
I filled a glass of water for you
from a dreamt up faucet
in this dreamt up kitchen,
bid you drink, but your body
began to crumble to the ground,
on hand and knee you disgorged
life into ash as the dirt
ungodly pulled you down,
toward darkness,
swallowed you whole
with no chance for mercy
as I watched helpless,
languid cipher in a dream,
and all I could do
was wake myself up,
in a panic, unable
to move, unable
to remember, beneath
a cold, gray morning,
sweat stained sheets,
a red comforter,
faded, torn,
unraveled.

Eastbound Twenty-One

My body on a twenty-one.
My body, an eastbound echo
of my father's, his own twenty-one,
our brown skin, scarred against
ragged blue velvet, upholstery,
taste of the transit god.
I imagine a throne, for poets,
fools, and sons, I am all three,
but my trinity is not divine.
My father, I am your echo, listen
for an engine just down the road,
before I fade, like all good echoes,
I will close my eyes and fall asleep,
Cash's "Wayfaring Stranger" in my ear
as we cross the milky river, I'll dream,
two white wings over the wheel,
we float, drift toward our final stop.
When I wake, you will be there.
You will know my face, my confusion.
My father, you will take my hand in yours,
        you will say *we're home*.

Gratitude

To no one in particular, as he walks lakeside
with an autumn wind, he whispers: *I am grateful.*

*Warm home, good job, sturdy coat, just enough
hope in the morning*, yes he is grateful for it all,

but he knows his gratitude would not exist without
its cold, lonely opposite, the voice that strives

at night for a reason to keep hope alive, aflame,
afloat when all the pieces go adrift, a voice

that has found itself hidden beneath his bed,
limp shadow unable to offer more than a whisper,

oh Gratitude, his lungs want to fill with a spell
that sends him back to a time when his grandmother

was only a phone call away, he still remembers
her phone number and how his mother would run

to lift the receiver until one day the calls stopped coming,
he can taste his grandmother's frybread, hot off a cast iron,

can hear the lid come off a batch of her pumpkin bars,
and in his mother's eyes he can still see how safe she felt,

she could be the mother she knew her son deserved, now
his lungs are empty of the words that could bring it all back

so you can be with him, dear Gratitude, when the year's
first snow tumbles down and angels appear, when lights

find their way to other families Christmas trees
and other families find their way to each other,

when a flurry of expectation becomes a blizzard.
Oh Gratitude, if you're listening, give him a hand,

your hand so he can't lose you, forget you,
somewhere hidden in the lines of this poem,

my desperate attempt to keep you near.

The Hands of Two Brown Men

Two strangers sit together
on a crowded bus, two hands,
years apart, find each other bound
by a journey east on Lake Street.

Both hands carry history;
one is scarred, rusted, split,
dried & wrinkled, a single leaf
left beneath the weight
of some merciless sun,

the other is embraced by light,
radiant like a fresh coat of paint
layered over four new walls,
across a sturdy frame, a home
to bless the broken soil,

both are a window, a reflection,
when a firm grip meant immortality,
now, his joints moan a prayer,
now, the water glass crashes down,
now, he will learn to let go.

Two brown hands on a bus
share their lives, all torn nails,
callused pads, quietly they teach
how to grab a punch, shape it

into words on a sheet of paper,
arrange it like food for another's plate,
guide it to an open palm's embrace,
an offer of peace dissolves the fist.

Two hands, their hands,
plan a revolution, crack knuckles,
tap to a rhythm only they can hear.
One hand reaches for the yellow cord,
the other waves a brief farewell.

In Winter Along the Weathered Curb

a patch of grass reaches up toward the sun,
a veridian chorus in life's praise, they rejoice,
raise their blades high, the emerald hallelujah,
they glimmer victory beneath a wraithful Helios.
Today, theirs is a celebration of the unexpected
for there was a time when autumn's surrender
meant death would drift upon them a pall of ice,
a lucent fall that buried tomorrow, yesterday.
How the back would arch as color faded to sepia,
how they would watch each other fall as if a plague,
wilted mother, father, sister, brother, neighbor,
lover who dived to follow another lover's dive,
the final curve and graceful exit from the field,
nothing left but a hush of bitter diamonds
until one day when death failed to descend,
no hellion's wings impressed upon the hill
nor cloak of winter tight around their crowns,
no frozen soil nor culm drawn to acquiescence.
Though some kept low, more stood taller still
as the heat refused to fade, their blades willed it so,
and they sang as they held themselves up to the sky,
to the heavens, to Helios and his wraithful glare,
and so it was that winter didn't fall that year,
so it was death would never claim the plot,
so it was a small patch of grass held green,
together, all along the weathered curb.

Mercy

My father, maybe I forgive you,
I'd prefer to not stay mad forever,
anger is a dangerous slope, steep,
all invisible ice and little traction
in a beloved pair of Doc Martens.

Too easy to slip all the way down,
dive headfirst to the bottom of a hill
Kate Bush sings about running up,
and down there every word I've ever
brought into this life about you

calling me into form and body,
your body though never your image,
still, too much like you, I can't unsee
all that keeps us father and son,
so instead maybe I forgive you,

in a way, offer myself forgiveness,
this only son who holds grievances
against the dead, it's no one's fault,
sometimes our hand is drawn
from a defective deck, the odds

in favor of what we've already lost,
and I need compassion like oxygen,
my father, I crave any empathy
for the no-longer-with-us,
for the thou-art-in-heaven,
for your broken hallelujah.

Now, I cannot reach you.
You are an empty, bereft space.
Now, I wear your name as mine,
sole inheritance, an online obituary,
yours, but too easily I see myself.

So maybe today I forgive all this,
place mercy on a debt we both owe
to ourselves and to each other.
It isn't much right now,
but it's just enough.

an exhalation

breath held close,
his lungs weep.

a verse of air,
a spirit's voice.

an angel stumbles,
wings dissolve.

his mother's halo,
covered in thorns.

his still mouth,
not a sound.

shadow of a boy,
the lightless corner.

close your eyes,
let this fade.

an echo,
a breath,

every word
an exhalation.

at dawn, bel canto
for Maria Callas

        i am told there is a will,
      if you listen closely at night,
     you might hear it sing,
    & sometimes i imagine
   the song of Maria Callas,
vissi d'arte, vissi d'amore,

an aria composed divine,
a voice beyond the stave,
the edge of my bed a shore
  as wave overcomes
    this collection of bone & muscle,
      blood, skin & teeth
    i have known as *body*.

      water reaches for water
        & upon the crest,
         there are no butterflies,
        only the swollen night,
          breath gone, lungs heavy,
         sharp with crystal salt,
          no man waits for the fall,

            who waits for me?

       flood upon the stage,
        there is a will,
         it gives itself away to dawn,
         it gives itself away to love,
         i have given myself away
          to men in hope of love,
        to mourn in hope to forget

        what ruin lays before me,
       what bell is never rung,
      & through the fog
      a silver ship arrives,
    at dawn,
   bel canto.

Listen, The Earth

Listen, I've heard the rustle
beneath paved roads,
the roots that reach, spread,
they gather themselves in the dark,
how even without a promise of light
their language remains illumination.
Listen, their council is an ask to remember
what life exists just on the periphery,
ready to flower in vivid saturation,
to speak, the sweetest tall grass,
to sing, the fragrant lilac chorus,
& the trees, the trees, the trees,
watchers of soil,
guardians of a scripture
only Earth knows,
not a secret but a privilege,
this invocation, this hushed hum
of river, of birch,
of cedar, maple, elm,
of willow, to weep no more.

Listen, this is the Earth,
her voice to guide us home.

Southside Coffee Shop
Minneapolis, Fall 2023

The poet in a café,
over cold coffee,
a turkey sandwich,
sits perched, stares
past the window glass,
onto the intersection,
Nicollet & 37th Street,
      in South Minneapolis
          & he wonders *did i blink?*
wonders why he blinks,
if something is missed,
not here, mid-blink,
it's just cliché,
the poet's body
of work will fail,
instead, the green paint
      keeps his eyes open,
          two buildings over there,
were they always so green?
the poet imagines color:
gray, orange, yellow,
billows of blue tarp,
maybe scaffold,
rusted, wrapped
around an echo,
      another mouthful,
        he forces a blink,
a poet returns his gaze,
deeper lines than before,
coffee colder than it was,
time gathered in a cup,
how long has he been
not right here, but here,
as his mother rings,
his phone on silent,

        this poem isn't grief.

River's Grace

Should it be the hour comes to pass,
the hour when our rivers fall silent,
the hour when our fathers turn away,
when our mothers put to rest the brush
and canvas, finally at peace in the swirl
of jade, indigo, emerald, ivory, at peace
with every color that lights our northern sky,
as we arrive to the edge of our final spring,
I will cup in my hands a crystalline prayer,
and drink of the water, the memory of Earth,
I will watch my body return itself gently to soil
and I will know, I will know we have lived as we
were always meant to live, in the full breath
and sway of summer leaves along the branch,
underneath the bloom and its crown of sun,
in the sweet of every moment's grace.

Good Night Hunter

Goodnight to you silver moon,
here is a red graffiti skull sprayed
against the hollow grain elevator,
and these, rows of illuminated teeth
that manducate over plot and land,
and this is a pale horse that blinks,
frozen beneath suspended emerald,
ruby, a watcher's two beams that leak
aluminum, mercury, into midnight.
Maybe you've brought me Death.
Maybe this is our lullaby of dissent.
In a dream a man, maybe he is you,
surges from below, from nothing,
he lunges, until, I wake, *up, up, up.*
Do I hear my own voice call out to you?
Is the safety of this sleep behind a door?
My mother cloaked in black and white,
ashen angel, rocks herself against him,
this Hunter and his maddog fellowship,
an extinguished candle, a ravenous owl,
the mercy of his everlasting song,
an echo in your cloudless glow.

River Call

River calls my mother,
grandmother, my father
no longer with us,
father thou art in heaven,
his son, my body,
their relative.

River calls my body
back to mother's earth,
my mother to her mother's,
when river was crystal, pure,
soil rich, home beneath feet
that danced along the river

calls, earth & animal,
sun, moon, tide,
blood & flesh,
my sisters, Gakaabikaang,
my brothers, the fish.

River calls,
can't you hear?

We are coming home.

Author's Note
(April 2025)

As the years pass, it has for me become increasingly important to write with a deep awareness of how much empathy and compassion I imbue into every word I place upon the page.

When I was younger, my words wore around their shoulders, more often than not, a fabric of pure emotion, born from a need to express anger, hurt, sorrow, pain, at the complicated circumstances from which my world was forged: poverty, addiction, generational trauma, the list goes on and on. It was only after enough time passed that I could begin to grasp the ways in which my own story was in fact part of a greater fabric, worn around the shoulders of my mother and father, my grandmother, the whole of our family, and that they too needed and deserved as much compassion, empathy and understanding as I did.

It is my hope with this collection that those efforts are as apparent as any line break, stanza or title.

Just as important is my awareness of how I move through this world: I am a first generation descendant of the Minnesota Mille Lacs Band of Ojibwe, from my maternal side. Because of a thing called blood quantum (if you know, you know) I will more than likely never be an enrolled member of her tribal nation.

I have my father's name to its entirety, save where he was a senior, I am a junior, yet I did not know my father, nor did I have until I was older any substantial contact with his family for reasons out of any one person's control.

These contexts, on top of being a gay millennial male in an age of digital dating apps (its own strange universe) have often left me feeling akin to a weather-worn autumn leaf tossed to and fro by a wind with and without intention. However, and again through that which only time can proffer, I have grown more and more comfortable with allowing myself to simply *be*. I am Anthony Paul Ceballos Jr., a former high school goth listening to Evanescence, Madonna, Tina Turner and Alanis Morissette on a beat up CD player, writing to keep himself from sinking, who became the adult goth (or as I like to say, a casual gay vampire of sorts) who listens to Evanescence, Madonna, Tina Turner and Alanis Morissette on a not as beat up CD player, writing today to keep himself afloat.

Lastly, I am in no way fluent in Ojibwe. The words in this

book that are in Ojibwe are here because they needed to be here, because the story could not continue without them, and there are times when the creative universe tells you to ask no questions, nor feel any obligation to give their English counterpart.

For translation, and much more, visit The Ojibwe People's Dictionary at http://ojibwe.lib.umn.edu.

Acknowledgments

If you are reading this, you are reading the first acknowledgements section I have ever written. Maybe it means you have read the entirety of this work, or bits and pieces, or perhaps you have started with this portion. Whatever the case, that you have spent time with my words, and have supported this book, is profoundly meaningful, and for *you*, dear reader, I am endlessly grateful.

This collection of poetry is dedicated to my mother and grandmother. Though our journeys, like all journeys, have been complex, each in their own way, it stands that I would not be the person I am today without them.

To my mother: With every ounce of compassion do I share this story. Love is boundless and eternal.

To my grandmother: Though she is no longer with us, something that breaks my heart to this day, I would like to think she would be happy. Though I have no idea of the threads that bind our universe, I am comforted by the thought that I might one day see her again.

To my dearest friend in this world, Sasha Suarez; for your endless support over all of these years into decades, for seeing the light in me at times when I couldn't see it in myself, for the inspiring work you do everyday and for the way it gives me hope in such a heavy world, thank you. I hold it all so close to my heart.

To Lynette Reini-Grandell and Venus DeMars: At the most critical point in my young life, when whatever faith my 18 year old self had in this world had been dealt a deafening blow, you both showed me and continue to show me all that is truly possible when we move through our lives with compassion and empathy, with artistic creation as a guiding lifeforce, with poetry and melody in every breath.
This world is so much brighter because you two make it that much brighter in all you do. Thank you for your light.

I would not be who I am today without the great support and spirit of Birchbark Books and Native Arts, owned by Turtle Mountain author Louise Erdrich. By the time readers have this book in their hands, I will have worked at Birchbark for 8 years! To this day I still look forward to every shift, to seeing my wonderful coworkers, to the wonderful customers whose joy makes my day that much lovelier. Chi miigwech to every Birchbarker, and to Louise for your great kindness and support!

To Heid E. Erdrich, for everything you have done and continue to do for Indigenous poets, writers, and artists, for your support in my own writing, thank you.

To Kim Blaeser for the joy and light you bring to Indigenous poets from all over the world, and to everyone I have met through Indigenous Nations Poets (In-Na-Po).

To Kris Bigalk, thank you so much for taking a chance on this collection and offering warmth, humor, and the kind of poetic guidance only you could offer! You saw a book where I saw only endless pages before me, around me, to the left of me, to the right of me, over there…

To Sun Yung Shin for your mentorship; Carolyn Holbrook for your generosity and warmth; to Bao Phi for everything you have done for the Twin Cities literary community; to Halee Kirkwood, Chavonn Williams-Shen, Celina McManus, for being the wonderful friends you are; to Patricia Francesco Weaver for being an amazing and understanding instructor when I was at Hamline; to Rosy Simas for your great encouragement through the years; to Katrina Vandenberg and Mary Rockcastle; to Gary Dop and the Randolph MFA program; to Layli Longsoldier, Kaveh Akbar, Rigoberto Gonzalez, and Diana Khoi-Ngyuen; to Susan Daub for your profound insights; to Janice Denny for the work you do with Native students and the guidance you offered me through my early college days; to Jessica Fajardo and your great empathy and understanding and for that day in New York which I will always carry with me; to Su Hwang for your spirit and support; to Kate Kysar for your graciousness, we *will* take that walk soon if we haven't already!

To the stellar, unequalled literary, artistic and creative community of the the Twin Cities, Minnesota and beyond; Mona Susan Power, Sherrie Fernandez Williams, Roy Guzman, Juliet Patterson, Judy R. Wilson, Mark Turcotte, Mellisa Olsen, Diane Wilson, Clarence

White, Hawona Sullivan Janzen, Sha Cage, Heidi Czewiec, Elizabeth Tannon, Ian Graham Leask, James Lenfesty, Ardie Medina, Jon Medeiros, Micheal Kiesow Moore, Andrea Jenkins, Morgan Grace Willow, Marie Olafsdotter, Kao Kalia Yang, Lisa Marie Brimmer, Merle Geode, Stanley Kusunoki, Rosetta Peters, JG Everest, Erin Sharkey, Marion Gomez, Paige Riehl, Scott Vetch, Winona Vetch, RC, Tim Blighton, Mark Tilson, Ted King, Paul Van Dyke, Mary Austin Speaker, Chris Martin, Dixie Trichel, Nell Pierce, Rahcel Netwal Guvenc, Meghan Malone Vince, Art Coulson, Sarah Cassavant and Subtext Books, Andrea Corich, Megan Lambrecht, D Allen, Craig Ruhland, Abdul Ali, Richa Nagar, Michael Torres, Amy Fladeboe, Donna LaChappelle, Maureen Shealer Zhao, Angeline Boulley, Cherie Dimaline, and Gwen Westerman.

To my wonderful Indigenous Nations Poets cohort; Kenzie Allen, Tacey M. Atsitty, Mary Leauna Christensen, Kalilinoe Detwiler, Kinsale Drake, Max Early, Boderra Joe, Halee Kirkwood, Manny Loley, Casandra López, Rena Priest, Ha'ǎni Lucia Falo San Nicolas, Kristina Togafau, Arianne True, Annie Wenstrup, Bonney Hartley, Chris Hoshnic, Sarah-Joy Milner, Tyler Mitchell, Ruby Hansen Murray, Sunni Parisien, Sareya Taylor, Anangookwe Wolf; I am beyond grateful for the wonderful times we have shared together through In-Na-Po, and I can't wait for more! To the wonderful In-Na-Po faculty; Kim and Heid, Elise Paschen, Jodi Vander Molen, TJ Turner, Joy Harjo, Denise Low, Esther Berlin, Rob Arnold, Gordon Henry Jr., Edgar Silex, Deborah Miranda.

I have said it before but will easily say again and again, my gratitude is boundless.

Thank you.

About the Author

Anthony Ceballos lives and writes in Minneapolis, Minnesota, where he can be found penning staff recommendations at Birchbark Books & Native Arts, a small, independent, Native-owned bookstore. In 2022 he was selected to be a participant in the inaugural Indigenous Nations Poets retreat in Washington DC, as well as their 2024 retreat in the Twin Cities. In 2016 he was selected to be a mentee in The Loft Literary Center's Mentor Series program. He has been published in *Yellow Medicine Review*, *Water~Stone Review*, *Queer Voices: Poetry, Prose*, and *Pride*, and the anthology *Another Last Call: Poems on Addiction and Deliverance*, among others. He has participated in and hosted a number of poetry readings over the years across Minneapolis/St. Paul. He has been a featured guest on various Minnesota Public Radio and KFAI-FM programs. He earned his Bachelor of Fine Arts in creative writing from Hamline University in St. Paul, Minnesota, and his Master of Fine Arts in Creative Writing from Randolph College in Virginia. He is a first generation descendant of the Mille Lacs Band of Ojibwe. *Glassful of Prayer* is his first poetry collection.

About the Book

Glassful of Prayer was designed at Trio House Press through the collaboration of:

Kris Bigalk, Lead Editor
Sophie Baker, Supporting Editor
Natasha Kane, Interior Designer
Joel W. Coggins, Cover Designer

The text is set in Adobe Caslon Pro.

About the Press

Trio House Press is an independent nonprofit press based in Minneapolis, Minnesota. We publish poetry and prose that moves, inspires, and encourages connection, empathy, and understanding, with a special emphasis on underrepresented voices and topics. To find out more about Trio House Press, please visit our website at http://www.triohousepress.org.

www.ingramcontent.com/pod-product-compliance
Lightning Source LLC
Chambersburg PA
CBHW060536080526
44586CB00012B/749